Tristan, Dylan and the Dream Machine

A bedtime book

By Micah Moses

Copyright © 2019 by Micah Moses.

All rights reserved. This book or any portion thereof may not be reproduced or used in any manner whatsoever without the express written permission of the publisher except for the use of brief quotations in a book review.

Printed in the United States of America

First printing, 2018

ISBN 978-0-6920771-3-9

Book design by Micah Moses

Book artwork by Ryleigh Schmitt

Once upon a time,

there were two little boys who had so much

energy and so many toys.

Early in the morning they were both really loud

just a jumpin and a yellin man they even woke the

cows!

Their parents woke too and boy I tell ya, they were tired as usual and they weren't doing so well because their poor brains were done. They stayed up too late and it wasn't even a date night, though they sure would appreciate one. Instead they were trying to get the twins to bed, which the boys happily fought at every step.

Of course right?

Any-whozical, Daddy rubbed his sleepy eyes shuffling the boys back to bed, where they were tucked in, resting identical heads. "But the sun just came up and we want to play, if we go back to sleep we might miss the whole day". "Now you're just being silly", Daddy laughed and said, "It's far, faaaar too early for you to be out of bed". Just use your Dream Machine and things will be fine, you'll wake up well rested in just a short time. "A Dream Machine Daddy, what could that be?" It's like using your imagination when you're asleep.

"Like what?" they asked. "What could possibly happen?" Well, if your bed was a race car your seat belt you'd fasten. When you go back to sleep you can be anything you wish just make up your mind and follow the fish.

"Are you ready?" he asked and the boys nodded yes their smiles growing wider, covers snug to their chest.

He moved in real close so they could understand then peeked at his watch and Daddy began…

When we dream so deep and fly so high we can hear a mighty roar,

it could be the wind but

then again it might be a dinosaur!

Stomping and bashing and thumping around and always on the run.

Just like the twins as their day begins and sounds like so much fun.

Or go ride the range and do something strange

like play Cowboys and Indians.

Then be a caveman, running fast as you can

in the land where time begins.

You can be a detective and be most protective

as you search for clues unseen.

You can spot all the trouble or run on the double

or do most anything.

Let's be a fair maiden or a knight on a horse as we hide or we slay all the dragons.

Then dine with the King and do noble things like help others along in our wagon.

We'll roam through the castle and fight magic battles, venturing along through our fable.

At the end of the day we can sit back and say we had fun at the mighty round table.

Or you can dream about the pirate life and treasure far and near.

You can hear the sails a blowin with your fellow buccaneers!

You can ride the waves and swim ashore ever sloshing towards the looty.

You pass the shovel then dig your hole and there ye find the booty!

Dig in a mountain like miners do,

with pick and dreams in hand.

Or work in a river so cold that you shiver

searching for gold that you pan.

Time well spent was time well earned,

pay attention because it will teach ya,

sifting through dirt day after day until finally

y'all shout EUREKA!

Splash in the mud, wash off in the suds then go climbing trees all day.

Fly kites in the wind and share with your friends always laughing as we play.

Be a red giant or tiny winged fairy or a character from a cartoon.

Go forward or backward, jump up and jump down or go rocketing off to the moon.

Putting on helmets and strapping on gear and moving as fast we can.

Driving around really close to the ground because now you're a racing car man!

Circle the track with the scene whipping past as cheering fans scream in the crowd.

We can't hear them now because oh holy cow the roar of these engines are loud!

You can drive a big truck or climb a big hill

and find yourself way up high.

Or make other things happen like be a plane

captain flying way up in the sky.

You can pilot a sub and plummet so low where

you'll be in the darkest deep.

Follow Vampire squid or the strange angler fish

both lighting the way to be seen.

Will you stay inside or go outside where you splash then track in the mud.

Or go plant a garden and work as a farmer growing taters we also call spuds.

You can fly in the air, you can be anywhere or be anything that you wish.

You can sit, you can stand, you can walk on your hands, you can even make friends with a fish.

Compose masterpieces and learn things that teach us that stories are wonderful things.

Then we all dance around and make funny sounds at the joy that our own laughter brings.

We can paint funny pictures, create silly songs or write poetry meant to delight.

Or we can be clowns just playing around until well past our bedtime at night.

You're exploring the world by using your dreams just remember it's all in your head.

Think positive thoughts and have happy dreams as you lay yourselves down in your bed.

Kids close your eyes and dream your sweet dreams, though remember to not say a peep.

So mommy and daddy can crawl back to bed and get just a little more sleep.

Shhhhh.

The End

To the Almighty for all His good gifts and graces

To Kim, Tristan and Dylan

My good gifts and graces

www.ingramcontent.com/pod-product-compliance
Lightning Source LLC
Chambersburg PA
CBHW042142290426
44110CB00002B/84